KING HENRY VIII

The tragedy of Henry VIII lies in the fact that those abilities which could have made him a truly great king were in fact to be his undoing. Encouraged by the adulation and flattery of courtiers and companions, it is hardly surprising that he soon acquired a sense of his own superiority over all his fellow men.

A promising future

RIGHT:
A terracotta bust believed to be Henry VIII as a young boy. Henry received a wide education and was said by Erasmus, the great philosopher, to be a precocious child.

Henry VIII was the third child and second son of his parents. He was not, therefore, born to rule, and it was for Henry's elder brother Arthur, born in 1486, that Henry VII worked so hard to obtain a Spanish bride. Under Ferdinand and Isabella the recently united kingdoms of Aragon and Castile were rapidly emerging as the foremost power in Europe. A matrimonial alliance with their rulers would add immeasurably to the prestige of the house of Tudor and demonstrate to the world that Spain accepted Henry VII as legitimate king of England. And so, in 1501, after lengthy negotiations, Catherine, the youngest daughter of the Spanish sovereigns, came to England to wed Arthur, the young Prince of Wales. Within six months of the wedding the sickly Prince Arthur was dead.

Henry, not yet eleven years of age, thus became the heir to his father's throne. His younger brother Edmund had died in 1500 at the age of sixteen months and his two surviving sisters, Margaret, married to James IV of Scotland in 1503, and Mary, five years his junior, were discounted because of their sex. No more sons were born to Henry VII and in February 1503 his queen, Elizabeth, died shortly after giving birth to a girl who did not long survive her mother. And yet the future of the house of Tudor seemed to be in very good hands. Henry was a fine sturdy lad who was already making a name for himself not only for his physical prowess but also for his intellectual accomplishments. His father saw to it that he received a thorough training in French and Latin, the diplomatic languages of his day, and he developed a keen interest in and a modest talent for music, with a positive passion for theology. It is difficult to deny that Henry grew up to be a talented and accomplished young man.

This royal paragon was only in his eighteenth year when, on 21 April 1509, his father died. No rival claimant appeared to challenge his accession, his kingdom was at peace, and the nobility were tamed. Henry inherited from his father a level-headed set of experienced councillors, and a credit balance in the treasury; he could look forward to a long and prosperous reign.

'... *extremely handsome; nature could not have done more for him* ...'

DR. DE PUEBLA, VENETIAN AMBASSADOR, IN 1519

RIGHT:
Prince Arthur, the eldest son of King Henry VII and Queen Elizabeth. His death meant that Prince Henry became Prince of Wales and heir to his father's throne.

Catherine was five and a half years older than Henry, a young woman of twenty-three now marrying a youth of eighteen, a difference which came to be critical later. She was considered to be quite a beauty, and was certainly very accomplished; Henry had every reason to be proud of his queen. The weeks that followed their marriage were filled with festivities of every sort and Catherine joined in it all as exuberantly as Henry. The court of the new king was certainly a gay one. Gone was the atmosphere of restraint and caution which had surrounded the widower Henry VII. Gone too was his careful penny-pinching, replaced by a generous liberality which seemed in contrast utterly extravagant. Young ladies of breeding with good looks and lively manners were always welcome at court to enhance the revelries with their charms, but the king had eyes only for Catherine, and made in those early days a very public parade of his affection for his talented wife.

LEFT:
Catherine of Aragon. Henry married her as soon as he became king.

BELOW:
Henry VIII's horse armour. It was probably given to him as a wedding present by Emperor Maximilian I.

BOTTOM:
Henry VIII processing to Parliament in 1512. The Tudor rose on the canopy was the symbol of the unity of the houses of Lancaster and York.

One of his first acts upon becoming king was to marry Catherine of Aragon, his brother Arthur's widow. The Spanish alliance that went with the marriage was too valuable to be lightly cast away. Henry VII and Ferdinand of Aragon, past masters of the diplomatic game, had haggled for six long years over the details of this second Anglo-Spanish royal marriage, and the problem created by the closeness of the relationship between Henry and Catherine had been dealt with by a bull of dispensation issued by Pope Julius II in 1503; there was no need to go into that matter again.

Relations with Europe

RIGHT:
King Francis I of France.

BELOW:
The Field of Cloth of Gold. In 1520 England briefly held the balance of power between the two rival monarchs, Emperor Charles V of Spain and Francis I of France. Henry VIII can be seen arriving for his famous encounter with the French king, and in the centre background they can be seen meeting in a large tent.

Abroad as well as in his own kingdom, in his relations with his fellow monarchs and on the field of battle, King Henry also cut a very impressive figure. It is true that his first intervention in the current European conflict, the English expedition to Spain in 1512, was rather disgracefully unsuccessful, but the memory of that humiliation was quickly effaced by the triumphs of the following year, the defeat of the Scots at Flodden, the rout of the French at the Battle of the Spurs, and the capture of Tournai and Thérouanne. In 1513 the Emperor Maximilian and Henry of England had waged a joint campaign against France. That he should fight in equal partnership with the greatest prince in Christendom was very flattering to Henry's vanity. The Battle of the Spurs, so called because of the speed with which the French are said to have fled the field, was a small-scale engagement whose outcome did not materially affect the balance of power in Europe, but it gave Henry immense personal

LEFT:
The meeting with Maximilian I. In 1513 the emperor and Henry VIII waged a joint campaign against France. This painting records their meeting (bottom), their subsequent conference (centre) and their clash with the French (top).

BELOW:
A suit of armour almost certainly worn by Henry VIII at the Field of Cloth of Gold in 1520. Both Henry and the French king took part in the jousting and tournaments.

satisfaction and convinced him of his own military prowess which he had no other opportunity of displaying in person until 1544. After all this Henry's international reputation stood high, and reached its peak in 1520 when his two great contemporaries, Francis I, King of France from 1515, and Charles V, King of Spain from 1516 and Holy Roman Emperor from 1519, competed eagerly for his support. England briefly held the balance of power between the two rival monarchs, and the alliance of England with either would almost certainly ensure the defeat of the other. 1520 was also the year of the Field of Cloth of Gold when Henry and Francis tried so hard to outshine each other at a series of meetings in a specially constructed pavilion on the frontier between France and the English-held pale of Calais. And it was the year in which Henry had two meetings with the Emperor Charles, one in England before he sailed to meet Francis, and the second at Gravelines in the Netherlands immediately after the Field of Cloth of Gold. There was much less ostentation about these meetings between Henry VIII and the Habsburg Emperor, but they were certainly more productive of goodwill, and the Anglo-Habsburg alliance which Queen Catherine, as Charles's aunt, represented in her own person, was very firmly cemented.

Defender of the Faith

RIGHT:
The Golden Bull of Clement VII which confirmed Henry's title 'Defender of the Faith'.

BELOW:
Sir Thomas More, one of Europe's leading intellectuals, became Lord Chancellor in 1529. He refused to acknowledge the king as head of the English Church and was beheaded in 1535.

In 1521 Henry added to his domestic, diplomatic and military triumphs a distinction of another kind which gave him equal satisfaction. In 1517 Martin Luther had written a protest against the sale of indulgences and nailed it to the door of the church in Wittenberg. He had also written several arguments against corruption in the Roman Catholic Church generally, and as his ideas spread throughout Europe a fierce theological debate had ensued. Possibly encouraged by Wolsey, Henry now turned theologian and author and produced, in his famous *Assertio Septem Sacramentorum* ('The Defence of the Seven Sacraments'), an answer to some of

Luther's controversial writings. The first draft may have been polished up a bit with the help of Sir Thomas More – the most famous Englishman of Henry's day, who enjoyed an international reputation as a scholar and was a faithful servant of the king. However, there can be little doubt that the book was in the main Henry's own work (and in later life he was to regret some of his statements about the indissolubility of marriage and papal power), and it became a bestseller throughout England and Europe. Pope Leo X's enthusiasm for the book was far greater than either Henry or Wolsey could have anticipated or hoped for. It was dedicated to the Pope, and on receiving it he read it keenly, deciphering Henry's handwriting himself, refusing all offers of help. The work did not rise much above the scurrilous level which at that time was thought appropriate to works of controversy but on 11 October 1521 it earned from the Pope the grant of the title 'Fidei Defensor' (Defender of the Faith). Henry and Wolsey had tried for years to gain for Henry a similar title to those given to the Most Christian King of France and His Catholic Majesty of Spain, and finally they had been successful! It was confirmed by the Papal Bull of 1524 and Henry and all his successors have borne the title proudly ever since. Truly the King of England seemed destined to excel in everything to which he turned his hand.

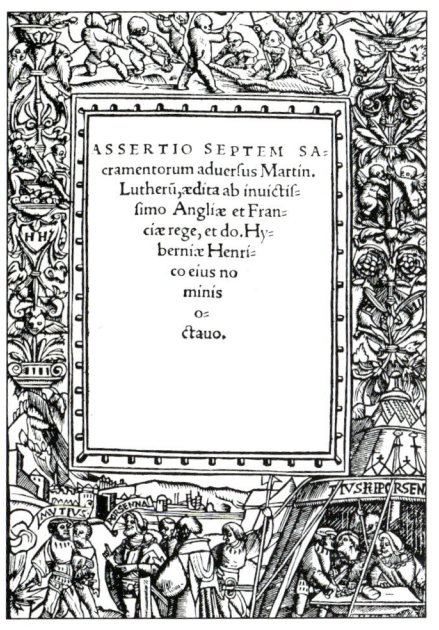

FAR LEFT:
The title page of Assertio Septem Sacramentorum, *the book in which Henry VIII attacked the ideas of Martin Luther.*

LEFT:
Archbishop Fisher who, with Sir Thomas More, helped Henry VIII with his book. Like More, Fisher was eventually beheaded for not acknowledging Henry as head of the English church.

Thomas Wolsey was born in 1475, the son of an Ipswich butcher. He was an extremely intelligent and able man and, on entering the church, he rose rapidly in rank. He became Archbishop of York in 1514 and persuaded Pope Leo X to make him a cardinal a year later. The king made Wolsey Chancellor of England in the same year, and until 1529 he was Henry's right-hand man, responsible for the day-to-day running of English affairs. Wolsey worked incessantly, his main aims being to achieve and hold onto great power and wealth. He openly sold bishoprics and, in terms of disposable income, he was the richest man in the kingdom – and Henry was a jealous monarch. In an effort to win back his king's favour, Wolsey presented Henry with Hampton Court, a palace of a thousand rooms, but it was not enough; when he then failed to solve the king's marital difficulties his days were numbered. He died at Leicester in 1530 en route from York to London to face serious charges which would probably have ended with him being beheaded.

The King's 'Great Matter'

OPPOSITE, LEFT:
Henry VIII had a good singing voice and is reputed to have written the song shown here – 'Pastance with good company'.

OPPOSITE, RIGHT:
An illustration from Henry VIII's own psalter, showing him playing his harp. Beside him stands his fool, Will Somers.

ABOVE RIGHT:
A delightful miniature of Princess Mary, daughter of Henry VIII and Catherine of Aragon. It was painted in either 1525 or 1527 and may have been sent to Francis I of France when Mary was betrothed to his younger son.

CENTRE:
Henry Fitzroy, the illegitimate son of Henry VIII and Bessie Blount. He was created Duke of Richmond in 1525 by a king anxious for a male heir. He died in 1536.

RIGHT:
Mary Boleyn, one of Henry VIII's two known mistresses. Mary was the sister of Anne Boleyn who became Henry's second wife.

1520 the disparity in age between the king and his queen was beginning to tell. She was worn down by repeated pregnancies and it was almost inevitable that Henry should have been tempted to infidelity. Just when Anne Boleyn first came on the scene is not easy to say and it is not until 1527 that we can say for certain that Henry had fallen for Anne.

Meanwhile, it is clear that the question of the succession had begun to worry the king. In 1525 he publicly acknowledged parentage of his illegitimate son, Henry Fitzroy, born some six years earlier, made him Duke of Richmond, and seemed to be preparing the way for making him his heir.

Here, in the king's dynastic anxieties and in his infatuation with Anne, we have the two principal reasons for his rejection of Catherine. It is hardly necessary to drag in Wolsey's diplomatic schemes. In 1526 Wolsey wanted to switch England from alliance with the Habsburgs to alliance with France, although Catherine consistently used what influence she had on behalf of her nephew Charles. To have had Henry free to take a French princess to wife might well have suited Wolsey's immediate purpose but would have involved the bastardising of the Princess Mary – for whom he was at that very time trying to secure a French husband. It is in any case

Yet there were disappointments also, even in these early years. Chief of these was the failure of Catherine to provide that much-needed son. Despite many pregnancies, the only royal child to survive infancy was Princess Mary, born in 1516. At first Henry had no reason to be unduly anxious, but the growing list of disappointments took their toll, and after 1518 there seem to have been no more pregnancies.

Henry, like most of the kings and nobles of his day, did not confine his amorous exploits within the bonds of matrimony, although compared with some of his contemporaries he seems to have been an exceptionally faithful husband. Only one illegitimate child of his is on record, and only two mistresses can be named with any certainty. However by

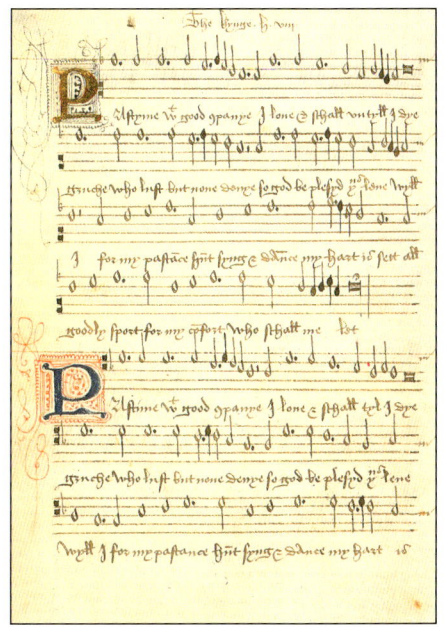

inconceivable that even in the fullness of his pride the great cardinal would have presumed to have taken the initiative in trying to pull down the queen. Once it was clear that Henry was anxious to be rid of Catherine, Wolsey could safely assist him, but he would hardly have dared to take the first step himself.

The long drawn-out proceedings in King Henry's 'Great Matter' commenced in May 1527 when the two English archbishops cited the king to appear before them and answer to the charge of having lived in unhallowed union with his deceased brother's wife. This was consistently the line that Henry took, that he and Catherine had never been properly married so that he was free, as a bachelor, to marry whom he would. Only the supporting arguments changed. At first he pleaded that the Bull of Pope Julius II, which had purported to remove the obstacle of affinity which had stood between him and Catherine, had been obtained under false pretences, and was invalid. At a later stage he argued, more sweepingly, that no papal bull, however correctly obtained, had any power to set aside the divine prohibition against such marriages as his. Only in the very last stages of the affair did he claim, reluctantly, that the pope had no power in England at all.

ABOVE AND LEFT: *Henry loved hawking, hunting and jousting and remained physically active until around 1530 when his increasing weight was already a problem. His hawk's headgear and hawking glove shown here are at the Ashmolean Museum in Oxford.*

Henry's Navy

ABOVE:
The scene at Dover in May 1520 when Henry VIII and his queen, Catherine of Aragon, embarked for France for Henry's meeting with the King of France.

Henry VIII's father was probably the true 'founder of the English navy' but Henry VIII transformed it from a handful of ships into a formidable fighting force. England, as an island, was dependent on her ships for both trade and protection; they provided the first line of her defences (apart from the northern border), and the stronger Henry's navy became the greater the deterrent it was to potential invaders. During his lifetime the first dockyard was built at Portsmouth, and the navy became a new and separate entity from the army, run by highly paid professionals, with a formal programme of development, repair and maintenance.

Up to this time ships had been used mainly for transporting soldiers and horses to war, and on the few occasions that battle was

joined at sea, the ships became simply fighting platforms with each side endeavouring to board the opposing ship. With the introduction of guns, everything changed and the warship became a specialised gun-carrying vessel. The *Mary Rose*, built in 1509, was remodelled in 1536 to become the first ship with broadside firing guns.

On 19 July 1545 Henry witnessed the loss of the *Mary Rose* when she rolled over and sank in the Solent. She had served the king in his French campaigns for nearly 36 years. The wreck was located in 1967 and is now on display at the Portsmouth Historic Dockyard. By 1547, when Henry died, the navy had grown to about eighty ships, and one of his greatest achievements was to hand over to his successors a strong and able defence force.

11

God's judgment and the break with Rome

RIGHT:
A miniature portrait of Henry VIII painted in about 1536 by Nicholas Hilliard.

While all these arguments occupied the lawyers and ambassadors, and while Pope Clement VII tried desperately to find a solution that would satisfy the English king without outraging Catherine's powerful nephew Charles, Henry and Anne had to wait. To have merely an illicit liaison with Anne would not have served Henry's purpose. He wanted a legitimate son, and he intended Anne to be the mother of that son. For that he was prepared to wait, but not for ever.

The more often Henry claimed in public that the loss of all his sons by Catherine was God's judgment upon him for having violated the Levitical law against marrying a brother's widow, the more passionately he came to believe it in private. And as time passed and the need for a son became more urgent, so he became increasingly convinced that a pope who could be so blind to the justice of his case could not be the Vicar of Christ on earth. Thus it was that Henry of England, *Fidei Defensor*, who had a decade earlier defended the authority of the papacy against the attacks of Luther, turned his own back upon Rome, married Anne, and excluded from England by act of parliament the jurisdiction of the man he now regarded as no more than one of the Italian bishops.

RIGHT:
Anne Boleyn. Henry VIII first fell for Anne in 1527 but they were not able to marry until January 1533. Anne was already pregnant with the future Queen Elizabeth I.

FAR RIGHT:
Henry VIII's writing box. Henry found writing tedious and usually dictated his letters, but he made an exception for Anne and wrote to her frequently during their courtship.

'I would you were in mine arms or I in yours, for I think it is a long time since we kissed'

HENRY, IN A LETTER TO ANNE BOLEYN

LEFT:
Thomas Cranmer was chaplain to Anne Boleyn and Archbishop of Canterbury from 1532. He always exerted a moderate influence on Henry and was the one man the king really trusted.

BELOW:
The earliest identifiable portrait of Princess Elizabeth, probably painted in 1546 when she was 13 years old.

He then arranged for his newly-appointed Archbishop of Canterbury, Thomas Cranmer, to declare his first marriage void and to confirm the validity of his second. In June 1533 Anne was crowned queen in Catherine's place.

Anne's marital history was for Henry depressingly similar to that of Catherine. Her first child, Princess Elizabeth, born in September 1533, was not the hoped-for son. Thereafter there were only miscarriages, and Henry began to wonder if there was not something wrong with this second marriage too. Thomas More and John Fisher, and a number of other distinguished men, had never liked it or the rejection of papal authority which had of necessity accompanied it, and they had gone to their deaths as traitors rather than approve what the king had done. Perhaps, thought Henry, he had been mistaken about Anne, or, more likely, she had bewitched him; he was not the sort to admit, even to himself, that he had made a mistake.

It was, however, the death of Catherine on 7 January 1536 which really sealed Anne's fate. Whilst Catherine lived any other marriage of the king would have been open to the same objections as that with Anne. With Catherine out of the way only Anne now stood between Henry and a third and undoubtedly legal marriage. A son might still have saved Anne, but in the same month that Catherine died she again miscarried. Already the king's eye had fallen upon Jane Seymour.

And yet it is difficult to understand the savagery of Henry's final treatment of the woman who had once meant so much to him. It would have been enough either to have executed her or to have declared her marriage void. Was it really necessary to do both? So complete was Henry's revulsion from the woman he had once loved so passionately that her death alone was not enough. He must free his royal person of all taint of association with her, even at the cost of bastardising her daughter and imperilling the succession. Henry certainly made a clean sweep of the past in 1536. When, on 30 May that year, he married Jane Seymour, he was, in his own eyes, a bachelor with no legitimate offspring.

An heir at last

BELOW:
A portrait of Henry VIII painted in 1536, the year of his marriage to Jane Seymour, mother of his son and heir.

BELOW RIGHT:
Hampton Court Palace, which Henry acquired from Wolsey in 1526 and where Prince Edward was born in 1537.

On this marriage, Henry's third, heaven at long last seemed to smile. On 12 October 1537 Jane gave birth to a prince, the future King Edward VI, and thus vindicated, in the king's view, all that he had said and thought about his previous marriages. Great was his jubilation, and for a few days all seemed set fair. Jane, however, never fully recovered from the birth, and on 25 October she was dead.

The death of Jane was followed by Henry's longest wifeless period in the whole of his reign. This in itself is a measure of the depths of his affection for his third queen. Her loss was a real blow to him and for a long time he had no thoughts of replacing her. She was, after those early idyllic days with Catherine of Aragon, the one he loved best of all his wives, and she is the one who shares his tomb at Windsor. Cynics, of course, will say that she

> 'Divine Providence hath mingled my joy with the bitterness of the death of her who brought me this happiness.'
>
> HENRY, ON THE DEATH OF JANE SEYMOUR

was fortunate both to bear him a son and to die before he tired of her, but, be that as it may, more than two years were to pass before Henry could bring himself to marry again. However, behind the scenes, the search for a new queen had begun.

This time Henry approached the question in a more orthodox fashion and sought to couple with marriage a diplomatic alliance with a ruling house. Under the guidance of

Thomas Cromwell, who in the 1530s took over the role of chief minister which Wolsey had monopolised in the previous decade, he eventually offered his hand to Anne, the sister of the young Duke of Cleves. Though the Duke was not himself a Lutheran, he was allied by marriage and by political interest with the house of Saxony, and through it with the wider league of German Lutheran princes. In 1539, since the Emperor and the King of France had for the time being patched up their interminable quarrel, and the Pope, Paul III, had seized the opportunity to declare his sentence of excommunication against Henry to be now in force, there was a real danger that the Catholic monarchs might combine forces in an attack on schismatic England. Against such a threat the German Lutherans offered virtually the only possible counter-alliance.

ABOVE LEFT:
Jane Seymour, Henry's third queen whom he married little more than a week after the execution of Anne Boleyn. The succession was assured with the birth of Prince Edward but the queen did not recover.

ABOVE:
Prince Edward as a baby, painted by Holbein.

The Anne of Cleves fiasco

> *Henry was struck to the heart . . . and had 'left her as good a maid as he found her'*
>
> HENRY, OF ANNE OF CLEVES

ABOVE:
A roundel of the arms of Henry VIII.

ABOVE RIGHT:
Thomas Cromwell.

BELOW RIGHT:
A portrait of Henry VIII at about the time the Bible was translated into the English language.

ABOVE:
Anne of Cleves. At the very time Henry married Anne he was already looking for a way out of the arrangement.

RIGHT:
Nonsuch Palace. Henry spent a fortune building and furnishing Nonsuch. Much of the money he spent came from the sale of leases following the dissolution of the monasteries.

The negotiation of a marriage treaty was, however, always a lengthy business, and by the time the arrangements for the Cleves marriage were complete, and Anne had come to England to meet and marry Henry, the need for the alliance which she represented was already passing. We need not accept as gospel truth all the unflattering things which Henry was later reported to have said about Anne in order to establish that he had never been able to bring himself to consummate his marriage with her, but we must accept that she did not fire his blood, and that once the diplomatic situation shifted in England's favour he saw no reason why he should remain tied to her for life. Anne was very sensible about it all. She made no attempt to resist the king's will or to fight for her rights. By her wise complaisance she earned for herself the title of 'King's sister' and a very comfortable endowment.

The Dissolution of the Monasteries

In the four years between April 1536 and April 1540 Henry VIII and his able administrator, the vicar-general Thomas Cromwell, took over the buildings and properties of more than 800 monasteries, religious houses, nunneries and friaries, which were then leased or sold to new lay occupiers. This major social and religious upheaval is known as the Dissolution of the Monasteries.

Great wealth lay in the monastic communities and the most likely reason for Henry's action was to raise money. The dissolution began with an Act of Parliament which transferred to the Crown the lands, buildings, furnishings, church ornaments, and all properties of any religious house with an income of less than £200 a year. Certain compensations were granted in return and initially many monks and nuns were able to transfer to other religious houses. However, after a small unsuccessful rebellion and the consequent forfeiture of some of the larger monasteries by the Crown, most of the rest of the monasteries 'surrendered'.

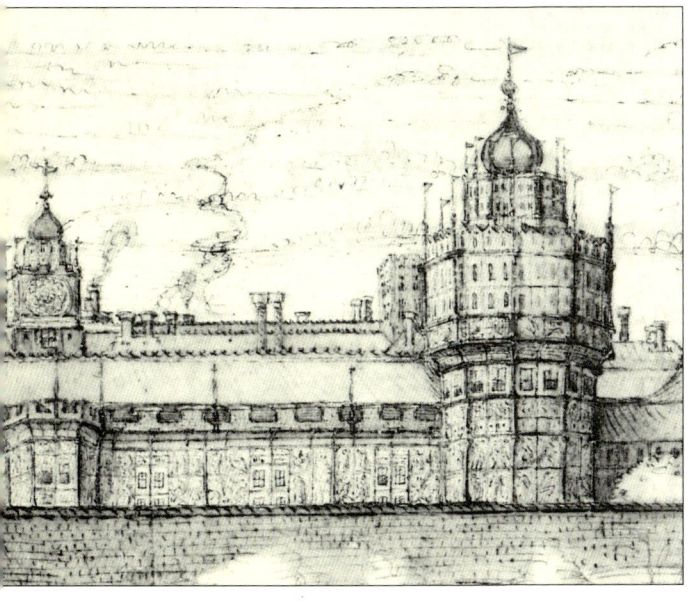

A monstrous betrayal

RIGHT:

Catherine Howard, Henry's fifth queen, was less than half his age when he married her in July 1540. She was so lively that the king was quite rejuvenated by her.

The story of Henry's fifth wife, Catherine Howard, is in many ways a repetition of that of Anne Boleyn. At the age of 49, and already talking of himself as an old man, Henry's passions were aroused and his spirits rejuvenated by the appearance of this girl of less than twenty. The king could not find words to express his admiration and joy when she consented to be his wife. She was his jewel of womanhood, his perfect partner, and much else besides. She was also, as Anne Boleyn before her, a niece of the Duke of Norfolk and the repository of the hopes of a political faction. She had been very deliberately put in the king's way by her uncle and Bishop Stephen Gardiner who were working to destroy the influence of Thomas Cromwell and to reassert their own. Anne Boleyn in her day had helped the promotion of many supporters of the Reformation, notably Thomas Cranmer. Catherine, they hoped, would in similar fashion be an asset to the conservative interest which they represented. Though Cromwell fell before the king divorced Anne of Cleves and married Catherine Howard, there is no doubt that the latter played an important part in bringing about this palace revolution.

Catherine thoroughly enjoyed her new position and the power and riches it put into her hands. She eagerly accepted the many lavish gifts bestowed upon her by the infatuated king, but she did not (how could she be expected to?) return his love and preferred, in a most dangerously indiscreet manner, to keep up contact with the men friends of her unmarried days. This was to be her undoing, more dramatically and more swiftly than in the case of her cousin Anne Boleyn. In November 1541, less than sixteen months after her marriage, a dossier of her indiscretions, prepared by her enemies, was put in the hands of the king by Cranmer. At first Henry affected to take little notice, but for form's sake started some enquiries. Before long the whole truth came out and the king's wrath was terrible. The idol was shattered; he had been most cruelly deceived by this flighty and unprincipled slut. He who had defied both pope and emperor had been made to look a fool. The very worst aspect of Catherine's behaviour was her total failure to show a proper respect for her royal husband who now, in his own realm, stood 'next only unto God' in authority over all his people. For this, as much as for her alleged infidelities, Catherine had to die.

ABOVE:

A suit of armour made for Henry in 1540. By this time he was very overweight.

RIGHT:

The lock from Beddington Place in Surrey, one of the royal manors. Henry would have held a master key for such locks used on his private apartments.

A need for companionship

FAR LEFT:
A portrait of Catherine Parr who married Henry VIII on 12 June 1542. After his death she obtained Edward VI's consent to her marriage to Sir Thomas Seymour.

LEFT:
Prince Edward who succeeded his father at the tender age of nine.

BELOW:
An illustration from Henry VIII's own psalter dated about 1540, showing him reading.

Henry's last wife, Catherine Parr, who survived him, was altogether more circumspect and deferential in her behaviour. She was older, and very much more experienced, than her unfortunate predecessor. When she married Henry on 12 June 1542 she was thirty-one and had already had two husbands, the second having been one of the leaders of the great rebellion of 1536 which is known as the Pilgrimage of Grace. She was aware of the dangers as well as the advantages of being Henry's queen, but she was wise enough not to oppose his imperious will, and skilful enough to know how to ease his suffering and to turn aside his wrath. In the closing years of the reign, while the political vultures gathered round the diseased body of the ageing king, and jostled each other for position, only she, and to a lesser degree Cranmer, brought any touch of humanity and charity to the faction-ridden court. She was a cultured woman, and was very much in sympathy with the Protestant reformers, but was wise enough not to appear too openly to be their partisan. Her influence was probably crucial in securing as tutors for Prince Edward men who were not only the foremost English scholars of the day, but were also to reveal their Protestant sympathies after Henry's death.

The death of Henry

ABOVE:
Even as Henry lay on his deathbed no-one dared to tell him how ill he was for fear of his anger.

RIGHT:
Henry VIII's will, affirmed on 30 December 1546. It set out clearly the line of succession – first, his son Edward (with the help of a Council of Regency), followed by Mary and then Elizabeth.

The precise nature of the disease or diseases from which the king suffered in his last years cannot now be determined from the rather imprecise medical evidence available, but it is clear that his latter-day obesity was abnormal and almost totally incapacitating, and that from about 1537 onwards he suffered agonies from an ulcerated leg.

On 28 January 1547 death came at last to Henry VIII who, during the course of his long reign, had sent so many others to the scaffold. Long after his doctors had despaired of his recovery his courtiers were unable to bring themselves to tell him to prepare for death, so mortally afraid of his anger were they to the very end. Consequently Cranmer, whom alone of all men the king really trusted because of his patent lack of ambition and all-embracing charity, was almost too late to administer comfort to his dying sovereign. Henry was past speech when the archbishop came to him, and could only press his hand in token of his faith. He left his kingdom, the kingdom for whose external security and internal peace he believed he had exerted himself to the utmost of his ability all of his days, to a boy of nine.

The great achievement of Henry's reign, view it how you will, was the cementing together of his kingdom under the unchallenged and all-embracing power of the crown. All else had been ancillary to this. The rejection of the papal supremacy had followed on, as we have seen, from the king's concern with his marriage and the succession, but a showdown between the king and the pope was probably inevitable in any case, and might well have arisen out of some other matter. Henry could not abide any rival in his realm. The Church in England would have to acknowledge his authority as effectively as did the parliament and other institutions of the state. Those who presumed to set themselves up as rivals to the king, be they native peers or alien bishops, were all struck down with equal vigour. The crown alone emerged triumphant, but by the time the process was at an end it was often impossible to distinguish the interest of the crown from the selfish will of a bloated tyrant.

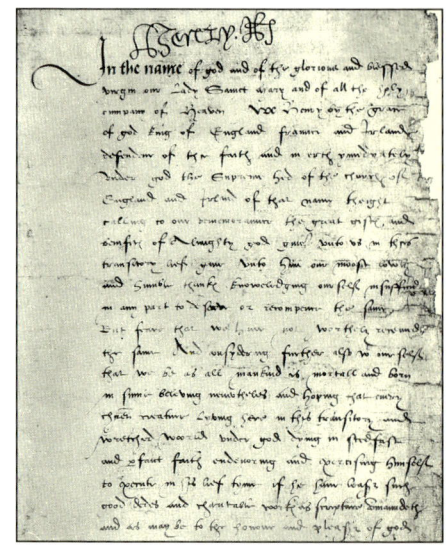

LEFT:
Henry VIII and his children, a protestant allegory of the English reformation. Edward VI kneels by his father's throne. Catholic Mary and her husband, Philip of Spain, are followed in by War. Protestant Elizabeth brings in Peace and Plenty.

BACK COVER:
The king in Parliament. A contemporary drawing of the scene at the opening of Parliament in 1515. Wolsey can be identified by the cardinal's hat above his head.

Acknowledgements

The Ashmolean Museum, Oxford: p.9 (centre and bottom right);
Bridgeman Art Library: pp.3 (top), 4 (top), 9 (top right), 17 (bottom);
British Library: pp.7 (top left), 9 (top left), 19 (bottom);
British Museum: pp.16 (top right), 16–17 (bottom);
Christ Church Picture Gallery: p.7 (bottom);
Hever Castle Ltd: p.8 (bottom);
Hulton Deutsch Collection Ltd: p.20 (bottom);
National Gallery of Art, Washington DC: p.15 (right);
National Museum of Wales (on loan to Sudeley Castle): p.21;
National Portrait Gallery: p.1, 6 (bottom), 12 (centre), 13 (top), 14 (left), 17 (top), 19 (top left), 20 (top);
Brian Pilkington: p.8 (top);
Pitkin Pictorials: pp.14–15, 15 (top left);
Public Record Office: p.6 (top);
Royal Armouries: pp.3 (centre), 5 (bottom right);
The Royal Collection, Windsor Castle, © HM The Queen: pp.2, 4 (bottom), 5 (top), 7 (top right), 8 (centre), 10–11, 12 (top), 13 (bottom), 18 (top and centre), 19 (top right), back cover;
St John's College, Oxford (by kind permission of the President and Fellows): p.16 (left);
Trinity College, Cambridge (by kind permission of the Master and Fellows): p.3 (bottom);
Victoria & Albert Museum (by courtesy of the Board of Trustees): pp.12 (bottom), 18 (bottom);
Walker Art Gallery: front cover.

Based on an original text by G W O Woodward.
Edited by Ann Lockhart.
Designed by Adrian Hodgkins Design.

Publication in this form © Pitkin Pictorials 1993. No part of this publication may be reproduced by any means without the permission of Pitkin Pictorials.

Printed in Great Britain by Cedar Colour, Eastleigh, Hants.
ISBN 0 85372 557 8   193/15

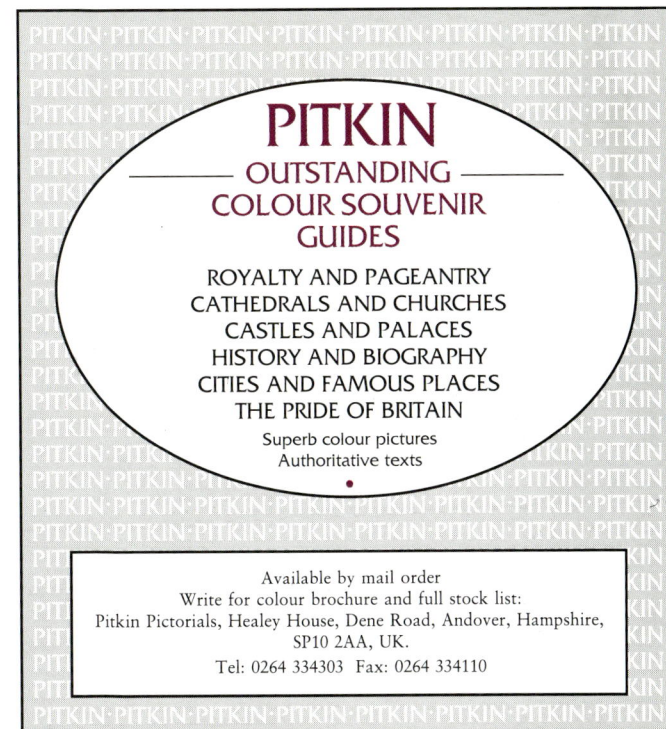

PITKIN
OUTSTANDING COLOUR SOUVENIR GUIDES

ROYALTY AND PAGEANTRY
CATHEDRALS AND CHURCHES
CASTLES AND PALACES
HISTORY AND BIOGRAPHY
CITIES AND FAMOUS PLACES
THE PRIDE OF BRITAIN

Superb colour pictures
Authoritative texts

•

Available by mail order
Write for colour brochure and full stock list:
Pitkin Pictorials, Healey House, Dene Road, Andover, Hampshire, SP10 2AA, UK.
Tel: 0264 334303 Fax: 0264 334110